A MOSAIC OF THOUGHTS

A JOURNEY THROUGH LIFE'S BOULEVARD

DR. SRABANI BASU

Copyright © Dr. Srabani Basu
All Rights Reserved.

This book has been self-published with all reasonable efforts taken to make the material error-free by the author. No part of this book shall be used, reproduced in any manner whatsoever without written permission from the author, except in the case of brief quotations embodied in critical articles and reviews.

The Author of this book is solely responsible and liable for its content including but not limited to the views, representations, descriptions, statements, information, opinions and references ["Content"]. The Content of this book shall not constitute or be construed or deemed to reflect the opinion or expression of the Publisher or Editor. Neither the Publisher nor Editor endorse or approve the Content of this book or guarantee the reliability, accuracy or completeness of the Content published herein and do not make any representations or warranties of any kind, express or implied, including but not limited to the implied warranties of merchantability, fitness for a particular purpose. The Publisher and Editor shall not be liable whatsoever for any errors, omissions, whether such errors or omissions result from negligence, accident, or any other cause or claims for loss or damages of any kind, including without limitation, indirect or consequential loss or damage arising out of use, inability to use, or about the reliability, accuracy or sufficiency of the information contained in this book.

Made with ♥ on the Notion Press Platform
www.notionpress.com

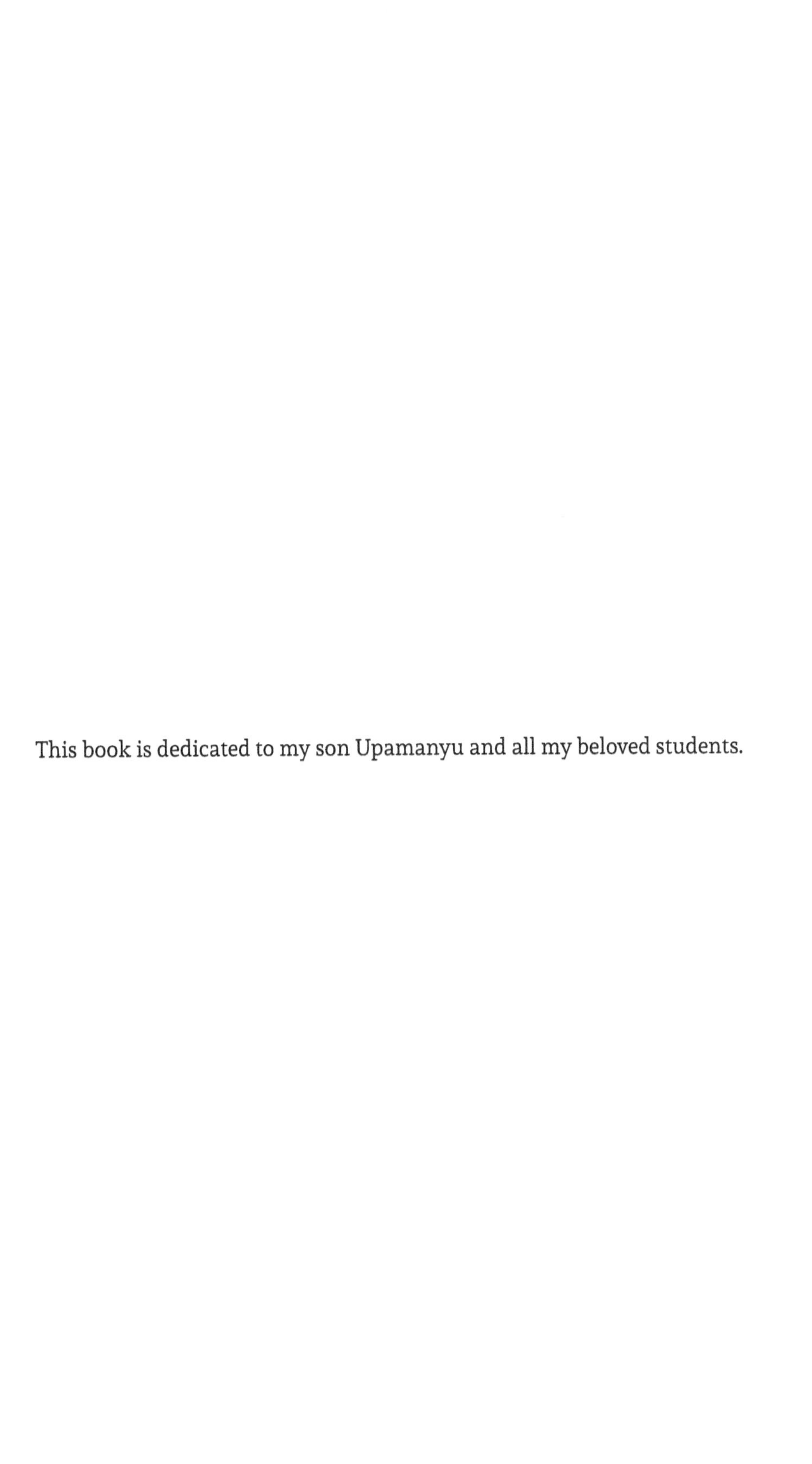

This book is dedicated to my son Upamanyu and all my beloved students.

Contents

PREFACE

Embarking on the journey of writing this collection of articles has been nothing short of an odyssey, one that has tested my endurance, creativity, and resolve at every step. As I reflect on the process, I am reminded of the Twelve Labours of Hercules, each article representing a distinct and formidable challenge that demanded meticulous attention, relentless perseverance, and a relentless quest for knowledge.

Balancing my dual roles in academia and the corporate world has been an intricate dance akin to walking a tightrope over an abyss. The demands of academic responsibilities—teaching, mentoring, and research—are relentless. Simultaneously, the administrative duties inherent in leadership positions within the workspace added another layer of complexity. Striking a balance between these responsibilities required not only careful time management but also a profound dedication to both arenas. Each day presented a new challenge, whether it was meeting deadlines, attending meetings, or carving out precious moments for writing amidst a whirlwind of obligations.

This book, a collection of twelve articles, is the culmination of my extensive experiences in both the corporate sphere and the academic world. Each piece is a testament to the lessons learned, the insights gained, and the wisdom accumulated over years of navigating these diverse landscapes. The themes explored are varied—leadership styles, the dynamics of blame games, the paramount importance of time, and the ethical quandaries of plagiarism, among others. Yet, they are all interconnected by the common thread of my personal and professional journey.

Writing these articles has been both a labour of love and a Herculean task. The process was often fraught with late nights and early mornings, moments of self-doubt, and the ever-present pressure to produce work that is not only intellectually rigorous but also practically relevant. The endeavour required delving deep into each topic, drawing on real-life experiences, and synthesising complex ideas into coherent narratives that would resonate with readers from various walks of life.

The insights presented in this book are not merely theoretical musings; they are grounded in real-world applications and observations. They reflect the challenges faced and triumphs celebrated in both corporate boardrooms and academic halls. From exploring the nuanced intricacies of leadership to dissecting the corrosive effects of blame games, each article aims to provide valuable perspectives that can inform and inspire.

As you journey through these pages, my hope is that you will find not only knowledge and inspiration but also a sense of shared experience. These articles are a reflection of the struggles, triumphs, and insights that come with navigating the complex interplay of academic and corporate life. May they serve as a guide, a source of reflection, and perhaps even a catalyst for your own personal and professional growth.

Thank you for joining me on this journey. It has been a challenging, yet immensely rewarding endeavour, and I am honoured to share the fruits of this labour with you.

Dr. Srabani Basu

Acknowledgements

I am deeply grateful to many individuals whose support and encouragement have made this book possible.

First and foremost, I extend my heartfelt thanks to Mr. Pankaj Belwariar, Director of Communications at SRM University AP. His unwavering support and encouragement in getting these articles published in various online magazines have been instrumental. His belief in the value of my work has been a driving force, and for that, I am profoundly thankful.

I would also like to express my gratitude to my students Aaditya, Shirshendu, and Srujana. Their persistent persuasion and belief in the importance of compiling these articles into a cohesive collection have been pivotal. Without their insistence and encouragement, this book might have remained an unrealised dream. Thank you for your unwavering support and motivation.

A special thank you goes to my dear friend and esteemed novelist, Dr. Shyamal Bhattacharya. His continuous support and encouragement have been a source of great strength. As a Sahitya Academy awardee, his insights and guidance have been invaluable. His faith in my abilities has inspired me to push forward, even in the most challenging times.

To all of you, I extend my deepest gratitude. This book is as much a testament to your support as it is to my experiences and efforts. Thank you for believing in me and for being a part of this journey.

FOREWORD

Crafting a foreword for Dr. Srabani Basu's remarkable book is a privilege that I approach with great enthusiasm. Dr. Basu, an Associate Professor of English at SRM University – AP, is a renowned academician, corporate trainer, and NLP evangelist. Her profound expertise in decoding language and unravelling the intricate nuances of human communication sets her apart as a leading figure in her field.

Dr. Basu's passion for language is palpable in every piece she writes. Her commitment to demystifying the complexities of communication has not only enlightened her readers but also profoundly impacted learners and professionals alike. This collection of her insightful articles delves into various facets of human life and the professional world, offering a rich tapestry of knowledge and perspective.

Having had the responsibility of sharing her work with the media, I witnessed firsthand the immediate and enthusiastic acceptance her articles received. The media's appreciation for her content speaks volumes about the quality and relevance of her work. Each article is a masterful blend of compelling topics, critical issues, hidden truths, valuable lessons, and powerful messages, all skillfully woven together with her expertise in language.

Dr. Basu's writing is both fascinating and deeply engaging, making complex ideas accessible and intriguing. As you immerse yourself in her book, you will undoubtedly be captivated by her ability to decode language and communicate with clarity and passion.

I extend my best wishes to Dr. Basu for her innovative ideas and initiatives. May her book achieve the success it truly deserves and continue to inspire and educate readers for years to come.

Pankaj Belwariar,
Director Communications,
SRM University AP

I

Are We Manufacturing Countless Bricks in the Wall?

In the year 1979, Pink Floyd, the famous British rock band, rocked the music world with their iconic track – Another Brick in the Wall, which was a scathing critique of the rigid and oppressive education system.

In the year 1901, Tagore founded Shantiniketan with the intent of going beyond the limitations of conventional education, and interestingly, way back, around 1803, William Blake, the English Romantic poet, visionary and mystic, wrote:

"…. Thank God I never was sent to School. To be Flogg'd into following the Stile of a Fool."

The line that joins Blake, Tagore, and Floyd is the oppressive impact that formalised education has on students.

Formalised education has a long history; however, from a modern formal education perspective, its growth began with the industrial revolution, which impacted the entire globe, and a strong need was felt to structure and standardise education to meet the industrial demands.

In the pursuit of inventing machines, man has successfully managed to mechanise humans. When laws mandated compulsory education for children, factors like attendance, curriculum, and examinations became standardised, and that was the beginning of the rat race. The journey from man to machine to rats is indeed something we took in our strides, and in this 'madding crowd's ignoble strife' somewhere, the purpose of education, which, according to Swami Vivekananda, 'is the manifestation of the perfection already in man,' was lost.

Long back in the early 19th century, Blake waxed eloquently on the restrictive education system that he considered a detriment to the natural blossoming of human creativity and spirituality. He severely criticised the overemphasis of reason over imagination. In his revolutionary work, 'The Marriage of Heaven and Hell,' he argued for the importance of integrating reason and imagination for a holistic understanding of self and the world at large.

In the early 20th century, Tagore, through the establishment of Shantiniketan, envisioned a world of learning that would foster learning through a harmonious connection with nature, diverse cultures, individuality, and freedom. It was the vision of a world where

.... Knowledge is free.... Where the clear stream of reason has not lost its way into the dreary desert sand of dead habits....and the mind is led forward into ever-widening thought and action.'

Tagore, in this poem, uses the wall metaphor to indicate fragmentation, a metaphor also found in Floyd's song that conveys the separation of the individual from the possibilities that make a human a human.

With the passage of years, competition became the buzzword. As competition gradually replaced the spirit of competence, generation after generation looked forward to the quantification of quality and progress or the success nestled within the confines of a rectangular piece of paper called a degree.

Can a degree denote or connote the holistic growth of a human being? This is the Hamletian question that we educators need to ask ourselves. The situation has reached such a state that stress among young adults is culminating in depression and suicides.

The time has arrived for educators to relook at and rethink the ways in which we are imparting education. Thanks to the NEP, which has emphasised the importance of ability, skill, and value-oriented courses to be incorporated into the curriculum. The fact that the NEP insists on value-added courses presupposes the lack of values, and how students are encouraged to inculcate values in their lives speaks volumes.

Both the problem and solution rest with us – the educators: do we create a space for the young learners to explore their possibilities, or do we manufacture 'another brick in the wall?'

II

Of Apes, Leaders, and Organisations

"...but man, proud man,
Dress'd in a little brief authority,
Most ignorant of what he's most assur'd—
His glassy essence—like an angry ape
Plays such fantastic tricks before high heaven
As makes the angels weep..."

These are the unforgettable lines from William Shakespeare's play Measure for Measure. Viewed from an organisational perspective, these lines can have a very meaningful relevance to the kind of leadership that organisations have to suffer, atleast once during their life cycle. The unfortunate ones suffer many a times.

Yuval Noah Harari, in his best-seller titled *Sapiens*, defines the word homo sapiens as 'wise apes,' It is interesting to note that Darwin's theory of evolution shook the world in 1857, in which he postulated that man evolved out of apes. Shakespeare compared man to an angry ape in his play, which he wrote way back in 1623. However, the purpose of this discourse is not to prove who called man an ape first. It is about how much of the ape element can a man of authority discard to evolve as a genuine situational leader.

Coming back to the context of organisations, everyone would unanimously agree that for an organisation to thrive successfully, effective leadership is required. The next question that pops up is, what exactly is leadership? Is it a role or a designation in which an individual can be anywhere in between an angry ape and a silent dormouse? Both ends of this spectrum can be unhealthy for any organisation. Leadership is not about roles and designations; it is about the attitude that one consciously displays in a given context. It is a journey where an individual exercises conscious behaviour to empower himself and the team leads.

Leadership in any organisation, whether corporate or academic, revolves around three key elements: Targets, Tasks, and People. Two prominent models shed light on leadership dynamics. The Blake and Mouton model gauges leadership through two behavioural dimensions:

Concern for People: This assesses a leader's consideration of team members' needs, interests, and personal growth while accomplishing tasks.

Concern for Results: This measures a leader's emphasis on concrete objectives, organisational efficiency, and productivity when tackling tasks.

These dimensions yield seven leadership styles:

The Impoverished or "indifferent" manager is ineffective, neglecting both systems and team satisfaction, resulting in disorganisation and dissatisfaction.
The Produce-or-Perish Manager, also known as "authoritarian" or "authority-compliance," prioritises productivity over team needs.
The Country Club or "accommodating" manager focuses on team members' needs and feelings, believing that a happy and secure team will perform well.
The Middle-of-the-Road manager tries to balance results and people but often ends up with mediocre performance due to continual compromise.

PAT: The Paternalistic style involves praising and supporting while discouraging challenges to the leader's thinking.

OPS: The Opportunistic style adopts behaviours for personal benefit, exploiting and manipulating situations.

Hersey and Blanchard's model outlines four primary leadership styles:

Telling (S1): Leaders instruct followers on what to do and how to do it.
Selling (S2): This style involves persuading and engaging followers in the decision-making process.
Participating (S3): Leaders take a back seat, allowing group members to actively contribute ideas and decisions.
Delegating (S4): Leaders take a hands-off approach, entrusting group members with decisions and responsibilities.

Choosing the appropriate leadership style hinges on the maturity level (knowledge and competence) of the individuals or group:

M1: Group members lack knowledge, skills, and willingness.
M2: Group members are willing but lack ability.
M3: Group members possess skills but are unwilling to take responsibility.
M4: Group members are highly skilled and willing.

Matching leadership styles to maturity levels, the Hersey-Blanchard model prescribes:

Low Maturity (M1): Telling (S1)
Medium Maturity (M2): Selling (S2)
Medium Maturity (M3): Participating (S3)
High Maturity (M4): Delegating (S4)

All of these sound good, theoretically. The key question is, are leaders in organisations conscious of the thin line that separates them from managers? Many times, leaders adopt a managerial role and get into the styles of micro-managers, rudderless boat captains, ghosts, conflict-averse, and sleeping cheerleaders. While this might seem like a minor shift, it can have significant implications for the organisation and its employees. This overlap can result in a loss of vision and strategic direction, reduction of creativity & innovation, decreased employee engagement, ineffective decision-making, erosion of trust and confidence, developmental miasma, and resistance to change.

In a frenzied pursuit to quantify and measure growth, leaders may end up in creating more competition and this competitive fever can intensify in creating more and more glorified rats racing and biting off the tails of those ahead of them to be at the helm. Organisational leadership needs to focus on competence. Once people increase their competence quotient, competition becomes just a word in the dictionary.

Our culture is founded on the principle of 'Vasudhaiva Kutumbakam' which means the whole world is a family. It sends out a strong message about harmony in diversity, and not on control and singularity. Once the paradigm shifts from competition to competence, organisations will witness a surge of inspired employees, who would willingly tread a measure for measure so that the entire organisation can dance to a synchronised rhythm.

III

Is Your Map Meeting Your Learner's Map?

Have you ever consciously or curiously wondered what constitutes your map of the world? In simple terms, a map is not just what you come across in the geography book; it also means an individual's perception of reality and cognitive representation forged and formed by zer environment, culture, beliefs, and cognitive processes.

While referring to reality, it is wise to consider that it is not the same for everyone. The concept of reality is very subjective. We know that the human visibility spectrum varies, approximately from 430 terahertz (THz) to 750 THz, and the auditory range spans from 20 Hz to 20,000 Hz. This validates that anything beyond these ranges is imperceptible to the primary human sensory channels: visual and auditory.

Aristotle in his celebrated work De Anima mentions the five primary sensory modalities: visual, auditory, kinesthetic, olfactory and gustatory. The neuroscientists added sixteen more to push the number to 21, however, due to the overlapping of some these were zeroed down to four major areas: Thermoception (heat), Nociception (pain), Equilibrioception (balance) and Proprioception (body awareness).

Eco-psychologist Michael J Cohen adds 32 more to push the list of senses to 53. He categorises these 32 senses under four heads: Radiation senses,

Chemical senses, Feeling senses (not to be confused with the Aristotelian kinesthetic), and Mental senses. Cohen argues that our identity as beings is deeply intertwined with our sensory nature. He emphasises that our human senses constitute a significant aspect of our essence. These senses have been bestowed upon us, not for mere indulgence, amusement, or ornamentation. Rather, they are inherent mechanisms meticulously crafted to facilitate our survival and prosperity within the realm of the natural world.

Neuro-Linguistic Programming, a domain that emerged in the 1970s as a collaborative pursuit of Richard Bandler and John Grinder, claims that people use their five senses (VAKOG) to create mental representations of their experiences. These mental representations are known as internal representations or "internal representations systems" (IRS). The concept of the internal representational hierarchy suggests that people tend to favour one or more of these sensory modalities when processing and storing information, and this preference influences how they perceive and respond to the world around them and how they remember, interpret, and communicate about their experiences.

If we accept that we process the information picked up by our sensory modalities differently, then our preferred learning styles are likely to differ from one another. In this context, it is obvious that a classroom consists of learners with varying learning styles: visual, auditory, and kinesthetic, the last being a combo pack of movement, feeling, touch, smell, and taste. Every individual has two maps, viz, the inner or mental map and the linguistic map. Alfred Korzybski, a Polish American philosopher and scientist, introduced the phrase "The map is not the territory" as a fundamental concept in his theory of General Semantics. He aimed to highlight the distinction between human perceptions, abstractions, and models (the "maps") and the objective reality or experience itself (the "territory"). This concept emphasises that our mental representations of the world are not identical to the actual external reality they represent.

The term "linguistic map," on the other hand, refers to the mental representation that an individual constructs, often unconsciously, to organise and comprehend language. In essence, a linguistic map serves as a guide for a person's understanding and production of language. The linguistic map may be referred to as 'mental grammar', which encompasses the implicit knowledge that speakers of a specific language have about the rules and structures that govern their language structure. This map is the dynamic interplay between language, cognition, culture, beliefs, and values, shaping how individuals process and make sense of linguistic information.

In the classroom space, one size does not fit all. Every learner is a unique individual, shaped by their experiences, preferences, and cognitive processes. To truly connect and engage with learners, educators must go beyond delivering information and ensure that they are meeting their learners at their "map." This metaphorical concept emphasises the importance of tailoring teaching methods, content, and strategies to match each learner's individual learning style, preferences, and needs. However, even before observing and calibrating the learners and identifying their styles, we educators need to be aware of our preferred styles so that unconsciously, we do not end up imposing our styles on the learners and, when they fail to connect, brand them as stupid, unmindful, inattentive, etc.

One of the key aspects of meeting learners on their map involves not only recognising and accommodating various learning styles but also allowing oneself to be aware of the diversity and uniqueness of patterns that one has. We educators can ignite our creativity in terms of designing and delivering the courses, fostering inclusivity, exemplifying compassion, and, most importantly, creating a space where every learner can blossom according to their potential.

Education is a dynamic and multifaceted journey, and successful educators understand that effective teaching goes beyond simply delivering information. To truly empower and inspire learners, educators must meet them on their map. As we navigate the complex landscape of education, let us remember that meeting learners on their map is a compass that guides us toward a brighter future for all. And to quote John Lennon: "You may say I'm a dreamer. But I'm not the only one. I hope someday you'll join us And the world will be as one." amidst its multifarious patterns.

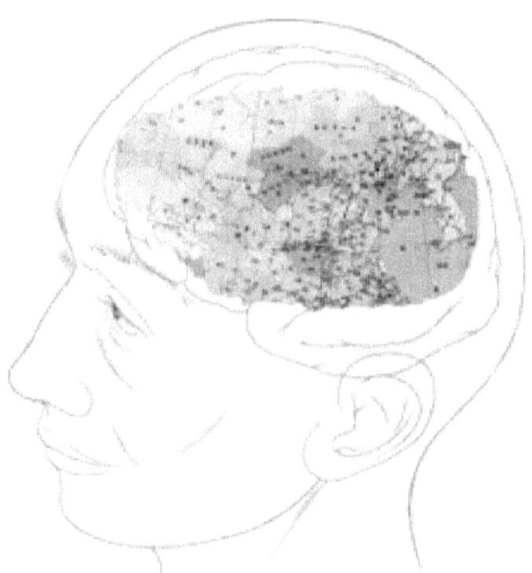

IV

Bullies of All Colours

Disclaimer: The word' colours' used in the title is a metaphor and has no resemblance to any form of racism.

The word "harassment" originated from the Old French term "harer," which means "to set a dog on" or "to attack." The word evolved over time and found its way into Middle French as "harasser," meaning "to tire out" or "to exhaust." The modern English usage of "harassment" emerged in the 17th century, primarily with the sense of persistently annoying or tormenting someone.

At the surface level, harassment may appear as one person causing physical, mental, or emotional stress to another; however, the intent to harass is deep-rooted. Without stepping into the realm of psychology, it would be worthwhile to explore the dingy alleys of harassment to discover the flicker of light at the end of this sinister tunnel.

One may perceive that in the grand tapestry of corporate life, where watercooler conversations flow like the mighty rivers of cubicles, and the air is thick with the scent of microwaved leftovers, that is where harassment breeds. However, in the wondrous world of academia, one may discover a place where the pursuit of knowledge dances cheek to cheek-with the fine art of workplace harassment. Very often, in the hallowed halls of higher learning, the air may be thick with intellectual superiority and the subtle aroma of passive-aggressiveness. The academic elites who hail from the chosen realms of premier institutes tend to look down upon their fellow brethren of different academic quills.

Both in the corporate and academic forests lurk several species of harassment, though this term has been equated only with the epithet 'sexual'. Let us not forget that at the workplace, bullying at different levels by different people is more rampant than sexual harassment and has nothing to do with gender. There is nothing sexual about a male boss reprimanding a male subordinate during a meeting, yet such behaviour comes under the purview of harassment. Discrimination based on gender, caste, creed, community, designation, disability, age and sexual orientation is a form of harassment. Abuse of power within organisational hierarchies, where individuals in higher positions exploit their authority to mistreat subordinates, is also a known devil.

Then, there is the new age of technology-enabled cyberbullying, which has ushered in the era of 'smart' harassment. Trolling, for example, is a trendy way to harass people. The keyboard warriors, armed with the power of anonymity, craft eloquent messages designed to make you question your life choices. Because who needs the drama of face-to-face confrontation when you can hide behind a computer screen?

Harassment, in its essence, is an unwelcome and persistent behaviour intended to cause distress, fear, or discomfort. It is a subtle and insidious force that can manifest in myriad forms, creating a toxic environment that corrodes the very fabric of social and professional interactions. The consequences of harassment are profound and far-reaching, leaving scars that may not be visible but are deeply etched into the psyche of the victims. From anxiety and depression to post-traumatic stress disorder (PTSD), the toll on mental health is staggering. In the workplace, the corrosive effects of harassment can lead to decreased productivity, increased turnover, and a toxic work culture.

The fight against harassment is not a solitary endeavour but a communal one that demands active participation from individuals, organisations, and policymakers. Creating safe spaces where victims feel empowered to speak out and seek justice is a crucial first step. This involves fostering a culture of openness, empathy, and accountability within communities and institutions.

It is imperative to remember that the fight against this pervasive issue is ongoing. It requires continuous self-reflection, societal introspection, and a commitment to dismantling the structures that enable harassment to persist. Albert Einstein said, 'The world is a dangerous place to live, not because of the people who are evil, but because of the people who don't do anything about it." By fostering a collective consciousness that rejects harassment in all its forms, we can pave the way towards a world where individuals can live, work, and interact free from the shadows of fear and intimidation.

V

Blame is the Name of the Game.

"The fault, dear Brutus, is not in our stars, but in ourselves."

This famous line by Cassius suggests that a man's destiny is controlled by his own choices and decisions in life and not by some luminous celestial bodies made up of hot gases that flicker millions of light years away from our own planet. How many of us are ready to accept responsibility for all our actions? We would rather prefer to wallow in the statement of Gloucester in King Lear: 'As flies to wanton boys are we to th' gods, /They kill us for their sport.' The happiest and safest feeling is to shift the responsibility from self to others.

For how many times do we spare a thought on the reason behind transferring the blame on someone else? It would not be futile to explore the psychology behind the blame games we play. Blame is a pervasive and often instinctual human response to adverse situations or conflicts. The psychological phenomenon of blame is complex and deeply ingrained in our cognitive processes, influencing our relationships, decision-making, and overall well-being.

Blaming others or oneself has deep evolutionary roots. Early humans relied on social structures and cooperation for survival. In this context, assigning blame served as a mechanism for enforcing social norms and maintaining group cohesion. Those who failed to contribute adequately could face exclusion or other penalties, making blame a crucial tool in ensuring cooperation within the group.

Psychologically, blame can be traced back to the concept of attribution theory, which describes how individuals attribute causes to events in their lives. According to psychologist Fritz Heider, people tend to attribute events to either internal (personal) or external (situational) causes. When things go awry, the tendency to attribute the cause to external factors often results in blame being directed towards others, while attributing the cause to internal factors may lead to self-blame or guilt.

Let us delve into the cognitive biases and their role in blame:

Fundamental Attribution Error: One of the fundamental mechanisms contributing to blame is the concept known as the fundamental attribution error. This cognitive bias prompts individuals to place excessive emphasis on personal characteristics or intentions when explaining the behaviour of others. In doing so, they tend to underestimate the impact of situational factors. For instance, encountering a driver who cuts you off in traffic may lead you to assume that they are simply a reckless driver (an internal attribution) rather than considering that they might be rushing to the hospital (an external attribution).

Self-serving Bias: Unlike the fundamental attribution error, the self-serving bias represents a different cognitive inclination. This bias leads us to credit our achievements to internal factors, such as our abilities or hard work, while we tend to ascribe our setbacks to external factors, like unfortunate events or circumstances. This particular bias serves as a protective mechanism for our self-esteem, allowing us to shield ourselves from self-blame.

Cognitive Dissonance: Cognitive dissonance theory offers insight into how individuals cope with conflicts between their beliefs, attitudes, or actions. When faced with such conflicts, individuals are motivated to alleviate the resulting discomfort. Blaming others can be a strategy for reducing cognitive dissonance, as it allows one to justify their own actions or decisions. For example, a smoker who develops health problems may attribute their condition to external factors like stress or genetics, thereby resolving the dissonance between their knowledge of smoking's risks and their own behaviour.

The Consequences of Blame

Damaged Relationships: Blame can erode trust and strain relationships. When people feel unfairly blamed, they may become defensive, resentful, or distant, hindering effective communication and cooperation.

Emotional Distress: Engaging in blame, whether directed at oneself or others, often leads to negative emotions like anger, guilt, and shame. The effect on mental health and comprehensive well-being can be severely compromised by these emotions.

Stagnation: Blame can hinder personal growth and problem-solving. By shifting responsibility onto external factors or others, individuals may miss valuable opportunities for self-improvement and resolution.

Escalation of Conflict: Blame can escalate conflicts, turning minor disagreements into heated disputes. When each party insists on attributing blame to the other, finding common ground becomes increasingly difficult.

The psychology of blame is a multifaceted phenomenon deeply ingrained in human nature. Understanding its origins, mechanisms, and consequences is essential for managing blame constructively in our personal and professional lives. By practising self-awareness, empathy, effective communication, and taking responsibility when appropriate, we can break free from the cycle of blame and foster healthier relationships, personal growth, and conflict resolution. Ultimately, a greater understanding of the psychology of blame can lead to a more compassionate and harmonious society where blame is replaced with empathy and constructive problem-solving.

Let us not forget what Eleanor Roosevelt stated, ***"In the long run, we shape our lives, and we shape ourselves. The process never ends until we die. And the choices we make are ultimately our responsibility."***

VI

Re-discovering Tom and Jerry Through a Quantum Lens

Albert Einstein, Boris Podolsky and Nathan Rosen would be rolling in their respective graves if they knew that their revolutionary entanglement theory was being compared to the popular cartoon Tom and Jerry. This beloved feline and rodent duo have entertained generations of viewers with their nonstop chase and slapstick humour. Prima facie, this classic cartoon may seem light years apart from the complex and enigmatic realm of quantum theory; however, at a closer look, one can trace the quantum-like aspects concealed within an animated world of mayhem.

It may be a rewarding exercise to peek into the world of Tom and Jerry through the curious lens of quantum physics. Entanglement is one of the most perplexing phenomena in the realm of quantum mechanics, and it challenges classical intuitions. At its core, entanglement refers to a quantum state in which the properties of two or more particles become intertwined in such a way that the measurement of one particle instantaneously determines the state of another, regardless of the spatial separation between them. In the cartoon world of Tom & Jerry, their destiny is similarly entangled. Their existence is intertwined in a perpetual chase where the action of one impacts that of the other almost immediately. This entanglement is reminiscent of quantum particles that share a mysterious connection, regardless of the space between them.

The observer effect is a phenomenon where the behaviour of observed particles is modified by the very act of observation. This phenomenon stems from the wave-like characteristics of matter, allowing particles to exist in multiple states simultaneously. When an observer conducts a measurement on a particle's specific property, they effectively collapse the particle's wave function, compelling it to adopt a distinct state. It serves as a reminder that the quantum world is inherently different from the classical world, introducing a level of unpredictability and subjectivity that challenges our traditional notions of reality and observation. Similarly, the audience's perspective and reactions to Tom and Jerry can influence their perception of the characters and the humour. The viewer's perspective can shift, making them empathise with either the cat or the mouse, altering their interpretation of the chase's dynamics.

One revolutionary feat in modern physics is the double slit experiment which demonstrates the intriguing wave-particle duality of quantum particles, their ability to create interference patterns even when sent one at a time, and the role of observation in collapsing their wave functions and determining their behaviour. This experiment underscores the fundamental and mysterious nature of quantum mechanics. Viewers of this cartoon would agree that Tom and Jerry, too, demonstrate a form of duality in their characters. Tom, the seemingly tyrannical and menacing cat, can sometimes assume a more sympathetic or even endearing role. Likewise, Jerry, the innocent-looking cute mouse, can become quite cunning and strategic. Just as particles can shift between different states, these characters oscillate between their roles, showing that appearances can be deceiving.

The unpredictable cat and the mouse chase can find its quantum counterpart in Heisenberg's Uncertainty Principle, which states that it is impossible to simultaneously know the exact position and momentum of a particle with absolute precision. In Tom and Jerry, we find a similar sense of uncertainty. The cat, Tom, and the mouse, Jerry, are in a constant state of unpredictability. No matter how meticulously Tom plans his strategies or Jerry concocts his escapes, the outcome remains uncertain. Just like particles in quantum physics, their positions and trajectories are constantly changing, making it impossible for one to predict the other's next move with certainty.

In the quantum world, particles can exist in multiple states or positions simultaneously, known as superposition where particles can exist in multiple states at once until observed. Within the cartoon's context Tom and Jerry often find themselves in a superposition of states. In many episodes, Tom and Jerry exist in multiple realities simultaneously. Tom can be both the predator and the prey, and Jerry can be both the escape artist and the troublemaker. This resonates with the concept of quantum superposition.

However weird or bizarre it may seem, Tom and Jerry and quantum theory serve as a reminder that even in the most unexpected places, we can find glimpses of the complex and enigmatic nature of the universe. So, the next time you watch Tom and Jerry's timeless antics, remember that beneath the laughter and mayhem, there may be a hint of quantum physics at play. Mr. Einstein, did I hear you chuckle from a parallel universe?

VII
The Irreplaceable Moments Explored

"Time travels in divers paces with divers persons. I'll tell you who Time ambles withal, who Time trots withal, who Time gallops withal, and who he stands still withal."
William Shakespeare

If 'TIME' can be perceived as an acronym, it can be expanded to ticking instants (of) man's existence. It is indeed the relentless march of moments which is a fundamental aspect of human existence. It shapes our experiences, decisions, and perceptions of reality. Yet, time is not a mere objective reality; it is also a deeply subjective and psychological construct. The study of psychological time constructs delves into the intricate ways in which humans perceive, experience, and manipulate time.

Quantum physics challenges the linearity, determinism and absolute nature of time. While quantum mechanics does not provide a complete theory of time, it has opened up new avenues of exploration and philosophical questions about the nature of time and its relationship with the quantum world. It would be an interesting exercise to move away from the mechanical concept and explore time from the philosophical and psychological perspectives.

To begin our exploration into the world of psychological time constructs, it is essential to recognise that time is inherently subjective. Two people can experience the same period differently, depending on various factors such as age, culture, and personal experiences. This subjectivity is exemplified by the well-known adage, "Time flies when you're having fun," or 'Time crawls when you're sad." This nature of time highlights the intricate interplay between subjective experience and the passage of time.

Psychological research has revealed that our brains process and perceive time in non-linear ways. One significant aspect of time perception is the "proportional theory," which suggests that we perceive the length of a period in relation to our total life experience. As we age, a single year becomes a smaller fraction of our entire life, leading to the common observation that time appears to pass more quickly as we grow older.

Psychological time constructs also involve the intriguing phenomenon of temporal compression and expansion. In moments of extreme stress or danger, individuals often report that time seems to slow down. This sensation is known as 'time dilation'. During high-stress events, the brain enters a state of hyperarousal, leading to an increased perception of sensory information and a rapid processing of events. As a result, the brain creates a more detailed and elongated representation of the experience, making it seem as though time has slowed down. In times of enjoyment and relaxation, the brain experiences compression, where individuals are fully immersed in the present moment, causing hours to slip away unnoticed.

Culture exerts a profound influence on the development of our psychological time constructs. These constructs manifest in diverse ways across cultures, impacting views on punctuality, the tempo of daily life, and the significance attributed to future planning. For instance, certain cultures favour living in the present and embracing spontaneity, while others prioritise meticulous long-term strategising and strict adherence to schedules. A fundamental distinction emerges in the contrasting perceptions of linear and non-linear time concepts. In Western culture, which predominantly adheres to a linear understanding of time, life is often perceived as a single, finite existence. Conversely, in many Eastern cultures, the belief in reincarnation takes precedence, reinforcing a non-linear perception of time, where life cycles infinitely through a series of rebirths.

Time, the constant river flowing through our lives, is marked by the various activities we engage in. From moments of solitude to shared experiences, our lives are a tapestry woven with threads of activity, isolation, intimacy, ritual, game, and pastime. Let's delve into each of these facets and explore how we spend our precious time.

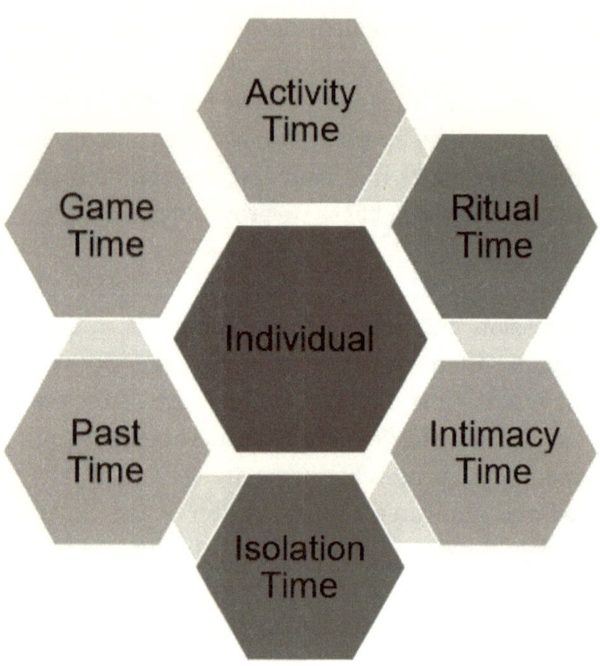

Activity is the heartbeat of our existence. It encompasses the mundane and the extraordinary, the essential and the frivolous. Activity varies greatly from person to person. Some find fulfilment in a fast-paced professional life, while others prefer a quieter, more contemplative routine. How we allocate our time in pursuit of our goals and interests shapes our sense of fulfilment and accomplishment.

Rituals are a testament to the human need for structure and meaning. They are often repetitive actions imbued with cultural, religious, or personal significance. Rituals can include anything from brushing our teeth to offering prayers. Engaging in rituals provides a sense of continuity and belonging. They serve as anchors in a rapidly changing world, reminding us of our roots and the values we hold dear.

Intimacy is the glue that holds our relationships together. It involves the sharing of thoughts, emotions, and experiences with others in a meaningful and vulnerable way. Spending time in intimacy can be with a romantic partner, a close friend, or a family member.

Isolation, often viewed negatively, is also a vital component of our lives. Moments of solitude provide us with the opportunity to reflect, rejuvenate, and recharge. In today's hyperconnected world, finding time for isolation can be challenging, but it remains essential for mental well-being.

Pastime is the art of leisurely pursuits. It involves engaging in activities for the sheer pleasure of it, without the pressure of achievement or competition. Pastimes can include hobbies like painting, gardening, cooking, or simply lounging with a good book.

Game time, according to De Bono, is a specific mindset or mental mode that individuals and organisations can adopt to facilitate more creative and innovative thinking. Game time is contrary to 'rock logic.' While the latter allows individuals to defend their existing beliefs and ideas, engaging in confrontational and argumentative discussions where the goal is to prove one's point of view as the only correct one, in contrast, "game time" represents a shift in thinking. It involves adopting a more cooperative and open-minded approach to discussions and problem-solving.

We are all familiar with the adage, 'Time is money.' Money is a powerful, tangible metaphor that signifies the importance of an intangible concept like time, as one can invest in, spend, save, or waste time through one's activities. The question is, are we aware of the ways in which we manage our activities to ensure an appropriate return on investment? If not, it's high time because 'time and tide wait for none.'

VIII

Of Halos and Horns: When First Impressions Go Out on a Blind Date

Tee shirt captions often carry profound philosophical insights. I once came across a tee shirt with the caption," You are only as innocent as the Horns that hold up your Halo." However, it may appear funny at the surface; at the deeper level, it carries rich imports.

Readers, I believe that you are not ignorant of the halo and the horn that appear on the heads of divine figures and the devil, respectively. In the wild world of human psychology, there are some phenomena that are as baffling as they are amusing. One such phenomenon is the Halo and Horn Effect, which sounds like something straight out of Dante's Divine Comedy script. But fret not, dear reader, for I am here to guide you through this peculiar journey of psychological bias with a humorous twist.

Let's start with the basics. The Halo Effect, not to be confused with the glowing headgear of our beloved gaming hero, Master Chief, is essentially the tendency for our perception of someone or something to be influenced by a single positive trait. It's like meeting someone who has a dazzling smile and immediately assuming they're a saint sent down from heaven to brighten your day.

On the flip side, we have the Horn Effect, which is the evil twin brother of the Halo Effect. It's when one negative trait clouds our judgement, making us see someone as a certified villain because they accidentally spilled coffee on our favourite shirt.

Now, let's imagine these two effects playing tug-of-war in our minds as we navigate through the circus of life. Picture this: you're at a job interview, sitting across from a candidate who looks like they just stepped out of a GQ magazine shoot. The Halo Effect kicks in, and suddenly, you're convinced they must be the next Elon Musk, Steve Jobs, and Tony Stark all rolled into one. "Hire them immediately," your brain screams, ignoring the fact that they just admitted they can't even boil an egg without setting off the fire alarm.

But oh, how quickly the tables can turn! Fast forward a week, and that same candidate accidentally sends an email to the entire company meant for their therapist discussing their irrational fear of paper cuts. The Horn Effect swoops in like a vulture, and suddenly, they're no longer the visionary leader you thought they were. They're just another mortal being with a penchant for melodrama and an unfortunate disregard for the "reply all" button.

Now, let's take a stroll through the dire straits of dating. Ah, love at first sight, they say. But what they don't tell you is that it's often just the Halo Effect masquerading as Cupid's arrow. You meet someone who looks like they just stepped out of a rom-com, and suddenly, you're convinced they're the one you've been waiting for your entire life. You ignore the fact that they still live with their parents and have a collection of porcelain unicorns that rivals that of a medieval princess.

But as the honeymoon phase wears off and reality comes crashing in like Lady of Shallot's cracked mirror, you start noticing the little quirks that were previously hidden behind the halo of infatuation. Suddenly, their habit of quoting Shakespeare during arguments isn't as endearing as it once seemed, and you find yourself questioning if they've ever heard of normal human communication.

Of course, the Halo and Horn Effect aren't limited to just job interviews and romantic encounters. They rear their mischievous heads in every aspect of our lives, from politics to pop culture. We idolise celebrities for their talents while conveniently ignoring their questionable life choices, and we demonise politicians for a single misstep while turning a blind eye to their decades of public service.

But fear not, dear reader, for there is hope in this sea of psychological bias. By acknowledging the existence of the Halo and Horn Effect, we can take a step back and examine our judgements with a critical eye. Maybe that person who cut you off in traffic isn't a heartless monster but just a really bad parallel parker. Perhaps that colleague who always seems to have a smile plastered on their face isn't a saint but is just really good at hiding their caffeine addiction.

So, the next time you find yourself falling victim to the Halo and Horn Effect, remember to take a deep breath, put on your best Sherlock Holmes hat, and investigate beyond the surface. Who knows, you might just uncover a hidden gem beneath all those layers of bias. And if not, well, at least you'll have a good story to tell at the next corporate training programme.

IX

A Comedy of Ctrl C and Ctrl V

'Non amo te, Sabidi, nec possum dicere quare:
Hoc tantum possum dicere, non-amo te.' – Martial.

We are familiar with the maxim, 'great minds think alike.' Have you ever thought that if Plato and Kautilya were to express the same thoughts during their times, would we still attribute greatness to their thought process or label them as 'plagiarus'? The word 'plagiarus' is the breeder of the word plagiarism. This word, however, has an amusing history. The Roman poet Marcus Valerius Martialis, aka Martial, was renowned for his epigrams. It so happened that a contemporary poet, Fidentinus, stole Martial's poems and passed them off as his own. Following this poetry theft, Martial accused his fellow poet as a kidnapper (plagiarius in Greek). This happened in the year 80 AD. Unfortunately, Martial could not sue the poem lifter legally due to the absence of copyright laws.

History says that Martial was not upset about his poems being stolen; he was perturbed that Fidentinus refrained from making any payment. In one of his epigrams, he wrote: *"Si vis ut dicant tua carmina, mittam tibi gratis. Si vis ut servant tua carmina, redde mea."* The translated version in English would be as follows: If you're okay with these poems being attributed to me, I will send them to you without any charge. However, if you prefer them to be credited to you, then please purchase this copy so that they are no longer associated with me. It is interesting to learn that ghost-writing was common among Roman poets to earn a livelihood.

From the time of the Romans up until the 17th century, the value placed on artistic skill often eclipsed the importance of originality, leading many renowned artists and authors to engage in acts of emulation and imitation. Even luminaries like Shakespeare, known for his enduring contributions to literature, borrowed extensively in the crafting of his most celebrated plots and passages. Likewise, the genius of Leonardo Da Vinci, responsible for some of history's most iconic works of art, did not hesitate to incorporate elements from the works of his predecessors into his own creations.

It is uncertain when the word plagiarism found its way into the realm of the English language. However, it is assumed that in 1601, Ben Johnson, the famous writer of satires, penned the word plagiary to denote literary theft. Despite all uncertainty of the entry of the word plagiarism, it can be most certainly said that in the grand circus of academia, where the nerdy lions and the scholarly acrobats perform death-defying feats with words and ideas, there exists a rogue character that even the clowns fear. It is an uninvited thief, incognito, who sneaks into the scholarly feast clad in the borrowed attire of the nouveau riche technocrat called AI.

Imagine a scenario where a UG student, a couple of nights prior to the submission of a term paper, with a pair of neon blue ear pods stuffed into each ear, stares blankly at the half-nibbled apple keyboard like a rudderless ship skipper, lost in the middle of the Atlantic. Suddenly, the epiphany manifests in the form of Wikipedia- not as a research tool but as a blueprint for creativity. Our overjoyed young enthusiast is inspired to copy-paste with wild abandon. At this very moment, the "unoriginal genius" is born.

In another location, a student has armed himself with a thesaurus, eager to dodge the plagiarism bullet. They engage in a perilous dance, replacing words with synonyms to make the text "their own." Little do they know that their paper now reads like a Shakespearean rap battle. Instead of avoiding plagiarism, they have unleashed the "Thesaurus Tango," where sentences go to die a linguistically convoluted death.

On a cold, brumal night, a harried writer whose fingers, trembling with a cocktail of stress and caffeine, accidentally highlights an entire paragraph from a research paper. The intention was to copy it to a reference document, but suddenly, that infamous misstep occurs: the "Cut-and-Paste Catastrophe." In a desperation to undo the damage, he pastes it into his own paper, hurling credibility into a tailspin.

At the core of this comedy lies a character who boldly claims the title of "The Master of Ctrl C and Ctrl V." This individual not only plagiarizes but elevates it to an art form. He constructs doppelgangers of published essays, articles, and occasionally the entire internet, all with the deft strokes of two keyboard shortcuts. He is convinced he has discovered the ultimate life hack for academic success, failing to realise he is in the comedy hall of mirrors where academic integrity meets bizarro-world.

In the academic Olympus, a curious phenomenon known as the "Distracted Detective exists." This character hunts for sources with all the enthusiasm of a bloodhound on a mission. However, his quest for the perfect reference often leads him down winding rabbit holes, and before he knows it, he cites a tweet from a parody account as a legitimate source. A comedy of mistaken identities ensues, and his paper becomes an unintentional farce.

And now, let us fix the spotlight on the "Plagiarism Detector Dilemma." Educators, with the best of intentions, employ plagiarism detection software to trap the culprits. However, students, clever creatures that they are, try to outwit these electronic bloodhounds by adding random symbols, emojis, and coded messages to their stolen content, turning their papers into secret enigma machines. It's a war of wits, where man battles with machines in a stealthy game of deception.

As we bid adieu to our cast of characters and the absurdity of academic misadventures, remember this: plagiarism is not a path to success. It is a comically tragic tale of shortcuts, misunderstandings, and misguided ingenuity. In the end, the only reliable way to avoid being a part of this tragicomedy is to embrace the noble art of original thinking and citation.

So, to all the students out there, when you face the daunting task of writing, remember the age-old saying: "To plagiarise is human; to cite divine." And to everyone else, let us keep laughing at the antics of plagiarism while striving for a world where academic integrity reigns supreme. After all, in the grand circus of academia, it is the originality that steals the show!

X

Echoes of Influence: A Caveat

"In the beginning was the Word, and the Word was with God, and the Word was God."
John 1:1

In an era where keyboards clatter incessantly, and social media platforms serve as digital soapboxes for the masses, the potency of words has never been more evident. From the trivial to the tremendous, every utterance holds the potential to shape destinies, alter perceptions, and even spark global controversies.

The adage "sticks and stones may break my bones, but words will never hurt me" seems more like a flimsy shield against the barrage of verbal projectiles launched daily on the battlefield of discourse. But perhaps there's a grain of truth to it, buried under layers of societal conditioning and self-defence mechanisms. For in the grand scheme of cosmic justice, it appears that every careless word carries a weight far heavier than the mere impact it has on the ears of its recipients. And when these words are marinated in different kinds of unpleasant tones and dished out to be consumed by the ears, they can scar a heart and mind for the rest of life.

As the scriptures warn, "But I tell you that men will have to give account on the day of judgement for every careless word they have spoken. For by your

words you will be acquitted, and by your words, you will be condemned"
(Matthew 12:36–37). Suddenly, that throwaway comment in the office break
room or that hasty tweet fired off in the heat of the moment takes on a
gravitas that can't be shrugged off with a casual apology.

The Bhagavad Gita, too, offers its sage advice on the matter, advocating for
an "austerity of speech" that consists of words that are "truthful, pleasing,
beneficial, and not agitating to others" (17.15). But in a world where the
allure of sensationalism and the temptation of trolling reign supreme, such
virtuous speech seems as rare as a unicorn sighting.

The Quran adds another layer to this already weighty discourse, warning
believers of the consequences of their utterances: "One may utter a word
which pleases Allah without giving it much importance, and because of
that Allah will raise him to high degrees of reward. Similarly, one may utter
a word which displeases Allah without thinking of its significance, and
because of it, he will plummet into the Hell-fire."

In the court of divine justice, it seems, there are no plea bargains for verbal
misconduct, no loopholes to exploit, and certainly no statute of limitations
on the repercussions of our linguistic transgressions. Every syllable uttered
into the ether echoes through eternity, shaping our fates in ways we can
scarcely comprehend.

But what about the corporate realm, you might ask? Surely, the power of
words holds sway in the boardrooms and cubicle farms as much as it does
in the realm of gods and prophets.

Indeed, in the cutthroat world of business, where fortunes rise and fall on
the whims of market trends and investor confidence, the spoken word
wields a formidable influence. From the CEO's rallying cry to the intern's
elevator pitch, every utterance carries the potential to seal deals, secure
partnerships, or torpedo careers.

In the high-stakes game of corporate communication, where clarity is
currency and persuasion is paramount, the importance of choosing one's
words with care cannot be overstated. A poorly worded email can spark a
chain reaction of misunderstandings, a hastily delivered presentation can

shatter investor confidence, and a thoughtless remark in a meeting can sow seeds of discord within the ranks.

In this relentless pursuit of profit and power, the ancient wisdom of the scriptures offers a sobering reminder: "By your words, you will be acquitted, and by your words, you will be condemned." In the court of corporate justice, as in the court of divine justice, accountability knows no bounds.

So, as you wade through the perilous waters of corporate communication, let us heed the warnings of the ancients and tread lightly with our words. In the end, it may not be the size of your portfolio or the prestige of your title that determines your success but the eloquence and integrity with which you wield the power of speech in the pursuit of your ambitions. Choose your words wisely, dear reader, for they may well be the architects of your ascent to the corner office or the catalysts of your descent into obscurity in the unforgiving arena of corporate warfare.

Randall Wright rightly asks: "Have you ever stopped to consider the power of words? Through mere words, wars have started and ended. Tender feelings have been hurt and soothed. Courage has been instilled and fear has been implanted. Lives have been destroyed and others changed for the better. Think back on your own life when words have hurt you deeply or have comforted and given you strength and hope to do better."

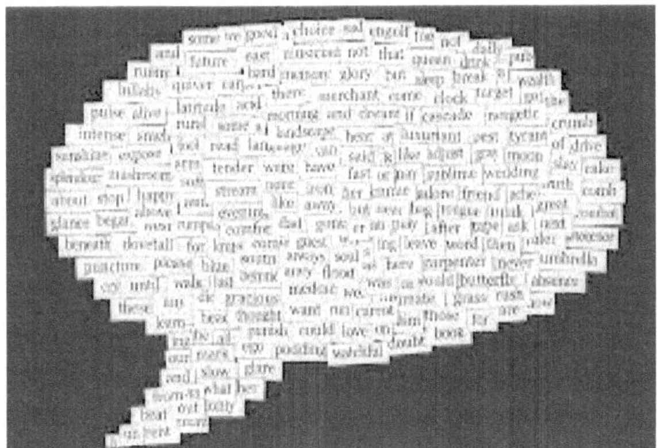

XI

The Parable of Corporate Exodus

"Nikalnā k̲huld se aadam kā sunte ayen haiñ lekin
bahut be-ābrū ho kar tire kūche se ham nikle."

(Tales of man's expulsion from paradise reached my ears,
But in stark disrobed shame, I departed from your sphere.)

These immortal lines, penned by Mirza Ghalib, sum up employees' exit from an organisation most poignantly. Most organisations become very active in retaining certain employees after they put down their papers, and in a jocular manner, these employees perhaps get noticed during their notice period. However, very few organisations take the root cause of such departures seriously and try to formulate remedial measures. Sometimes, people join and leave silently, and the management does not pay any heed.

Let us not forget that organisations cannot run on their own. It is run by people who have somatic and cognitive responses to the way they are treated within the workspace. The word organisation is derived from the Greek 'organon,' which means organ. From a biological perspective, an organ is defined as a collection of tissues networked in a particular way to serve a specific function. In terms of music, the word organ signifies a keyboard instrument consisting of several pipe divisions to create tones that produce a symphonic effect when played. These definitions, coming from diverse disciplines, point at one distinctive commonality, and that is arriving at a collective goal. No organ can function in isolation. There needs to be a harmony in diversity. And people in any organisation can work harmoniously when diversity is given its due respect.

There is a saying that 'people don't leave organisations; they leave their managers.' That is true, but the most appropriate deduction could be that people leave because of the feeling they experience at the hands of the people in authority. The common assumption is that people leave their jobs for money, workplace environment, desired career growth, etc. Well, all of this is true at the surface level, but at a deeper level, it is a very intense, unpleasant feeling that compels one to quit. Whenever a significant unpleasant emotional event happens, what an individual experiences is a particular feeling associated with the experience of that event.

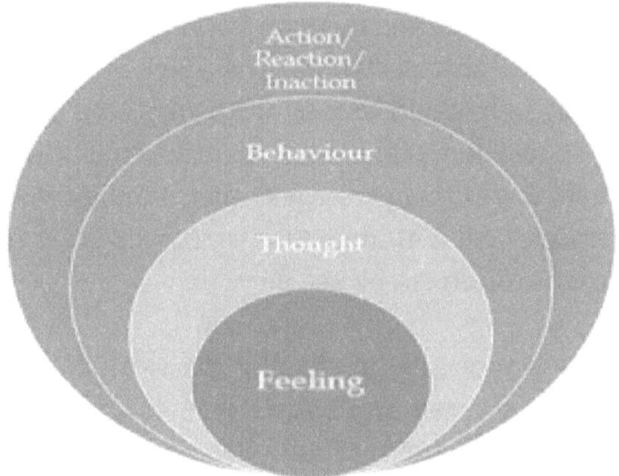

At the core there is a feeling that triggers a thought which in turn triggers a behaviour. This behaviour, in the case of an unresourceful thought often culminates in reaction and goads one to take an action which is, finding an exit from the space that is no longer considered to contribute to the individual's safety, comfort or growth.

Let us turn our attention to the reasons for attrition. One of the reasons employees decide to move on is the perception of limited career growth within their current organisation. When individuals feel that their professional development has hit a plateau, they are more likely to seek opportunities elsewhere. Companies that fail to invest in motivating through training programmes, mentorship, and clear career advancement paths may find themselves grappling with higher attrition rates.

Money matters and inadequate compensation remains a significant driver of attrition. When employees perceive that their skills and contributions are not adequately rewarded, they become more susceptible to exploring job opportunities that offer better financial packages. Competitive salary structures, performance bonuses, and comprehensive benefits play a pivotal role in retaining efficient and resourceful employees.

In the modern workplace, the importance of a healthy work-life balance cannot be overstated. Employees increasingly prioritise jobs that allow them to maintain equilibrium between their professional and personal lives. Long working hours, unrealistic expectations, and a lack of flexibility can lead to burnout, prompting individuals to seek alternative employment that offers a better balance. In fact, individuals work hard for their families, and when excessive workload forces them to neglect their families, their stress levels are bound to increase, and within no time, stress slips into the dark realms of distress. In order to de-stress, people move on.

Leadership plays a pivotal role in shaping the work environment. When employees feel disconnected from their leaders or perceive a lack of transparency, trust erodes, and attrition rates rise. When leaders within an organisation choose control over compassion, the chances of attrition shoot up. Leaders need to know what drives their team members. Not everyone's motivational drive is the same. It is wise to know that one size does not fit all. Money may not be every employee's primary motivation. Some may get motivated by recognition and appreciation. The most important thing that any management needs to remember is humans are beings and not a resource. An individual can become what ze aspires to be with the kind of motivation that is most appropriate to zer.

The culture within an organisation can either be a driving force or a deterrent when it comes to retaining talent. An unhealthy or toxic work culture, characterised by discrimination, harassment, or a lack of inclusivity, can be a significant factor in attrition. Employees are more likely to leave an organisation where they feel undervalued or where their well-being is compromised. Recognition and feedback are powerful motivators. Employees who feel their hard work and achievements go unnoticed may become disengaged and demotivated. Regular feedback, acknowledgement of accomplishments, and a culture of appreciation can go a long way in retaining employees and boosting morale.

In a rapidly evolving job market, employees often seek roles that offer long-term stability and security. Organisations that fail to provide a clear vision for the future and a sense of job stability may witness higher attrition rates. Career stability, encompassing both individual job security and the stability of the organisation, is a crucial factor in employee retention.

And last but definitely not the least is when what is preached is not practised. Employees are more likely to stay with an organisation when they align with its values and mission. If there is a perceived disconnect between personal values and those of the organisation, employees may feel a lack of purpose and seek employment elsewhere.

All the above factors are reasons for attrition at a surface level only, but at the very heart of it, there is either a feeling of insecurity, discomfort, frustration, dejection, humiliation or suffocation. If the leaders at the top put in that extra effort to know their internal customers well, not only from their ability or efficiency quotient but also what makes them happy, then most organisations can become healthy and a happy place to work.

XII

The Quirky Constellations of Human Nature

"People are like stained-glass windows. They sparkle and shine when the sun is out, but when the darkness sets in, their true beauty is revealed only if there is a light from within." - Elisabeth Kübler-Ross

Ah, human nature, a perplexing tapestry of quirks, contradictions, and surprises. It's like navigating through a bustling marketplace where every individual is a unique stall selling their own brand of eccentricity. As we stroll through this metaphorical marketplace, let's take a moment to appreciate the peculiarities of human behaviour akin to various everyday objects.

Some individuals resemble the Eno fruit salt. They burst into our lives with an infectious energy akin to the effervescence that greets water. Their enthusiasm is palpable, their presence electrifying. Yet, much like the fleeting fizz of the Eno, their excitement dissipated as swiftly as it arrived, leaving us wondering if it was all just a temporary spectacle.

Then there are those who are akin to eclairs. Just like the candy with its two layers, they present themselves in dual personas. Initially charming and appealing, they soon reveal a stickiness that clings to us uncomfortably, causing irritation and inconvenience. Much like trying to enjoy an eclair while battling the adhesive discomfort, interacting with them becomes a test of patience and dental fortitude.

Ah, the common flu personalities. They seem to pop up incessantly, like an unwelcome guest who never got the memo about staying away. With their arrival comes a flurry of discomfort – blocked noses, running noses, and aches aplenty. No matter how hard we try to evade them, they always manage to find a way to make their presence felt, leaving us longing for the day they finally bid us adieu.

And then there are those who resemble chewing gum. They come in various flavours, each promising a unique experience. Initially, they provide a burst of sweetness, tantalising our taste buds and leaving us craving more. But as time passes, the flavour fades, leaving us in a quandary – do we continue chewing, hoping for a resurgence of sweetness, or do we spit them out and move on?

Ah, the Indian gooseberry, or amla, personalities. Not the most palatable at first encounter, they require a catalyst to unlock their hidden sweetness. Like the amla needing water to bring out its sugary essence, these individuals need the right circumstances to showcase their true colours. Once the conditions are right, however, they reveal a delightful sweetness that takes us by surprise, leaving us wondering how we ever doubted their potential.

On the flip side, we encounter those who resemble big, polished green chillies. They exude an irresistible allure, tempting us with their glossy exterior. But much like taking a bite into one of these fiery peppers, our initial attraction soon gives way to a bitter taste, leaving us regretting our impulsive curiosity.

And let's not forget about the tiny yet formidable Carolina Reaper chillies. At first glance, they may seem innocuous, but one bite is all it takes to unleash a torrent of fiery agony that leaves us scrambling for relief. Much like these potent peppers, interacting with such individuals can leave us reeling for days, desperately seeking solace from the searing discomfort they leave in their wake.

Finally, we come across the dandelions of human nature. Fragile and fleeting, they drift through life like a gentle breeze, their presence ephemeral yet enchanting. Just as we begin to appreciate their beauty, they are whisked away by the whims of fate, leaving us longing for just one more moment in their company.

So, as we meander through the bustling marketplace of human nature, let us spare a moment to ponder the constellation of personalities that surround us. Each one is unique, each one quirky, and each one adds its own flavour to the rich tapestry of human experience. Embrace the diversity, cherish the eccentricities, and revel in the delightful unpredictability of it all. While the kaleidoscope of human nature keeps life endlessly entertaining, it's imperative to discern the individuals who form our respective constellations. In this context, it's apt to recall Oscar Wilde's words: 'Some cause happiness wherever they go; others whenever they go.'

www.ingramcontent.com/pod-product-compliance
Lightning Source LLC
Chambersburg PA
CBHW031243130726

47988CB00008B/3210